LOCKED UP FOR

FREEDOM

CIVIL RIGHTS PROTESTERS AT THE LEESBURG STOCKADE

HEATHER E. SCHWARTZ

M Millbrook Press · Minneapolis

To my husband, Philip,
whose love and support makes all things possible.

The author expresses deep appreciation to Barbara Jean Daniels, Carolyn DeLoatch, Robertiena F. Fletcher, LuLu M. Westbrook Griffin, Sam Mahone, Emma J. Pope, Lorena Barnum Sabbs, Juanita F. Wilson, and Danny Lyon for sharing their memories and experiences—and to Danny Lyon for contributing his photographs. Making this book would not have been possible without you.

The publisher gratefully acknowledges Dr. Charissa Threat, Assistant Professor of History, Spelman College, for reviewing and offering feedback on the text.

Millbrook Press
A division of Lerner Publishing Group, Inc.
241 First Avenue North
Minneapolis, MN 55401 USA

For reading levels and more information, look up this title at www.lernerbooks.com.

Main body text set in Bembo Std 12/16. Typeface provided by Monotype Typography.

Library of Congress Cataloging-in-Publication Data

Names: Schwartz, Heather E., author.
Title: Locked up for freedom : civil rights protesters at the Leesburg Stockade / by Heather E. Schwartz.
Other titles: Civil rights protesters at the Leesburg Stockade
Description: Minneapolis : Millbrook Press, [2017] | Includes bibliographical references and index. | Summary: "In 1963, more than 30 African American girls, ages 14–16, were arrested for taking part in Civil Rights protests in Americus, Georgia. Then came a greater ordeal: confinement in a Civil-War-era stockade."—Provided by publisher. | Audience: Grades 4–6. | Audience: Ages 10–14.
Identifiers: LCCN 2016036953 (print) | LCCN 2016058932 (ebook) | ISBN 9781467785976 (library binding : alk. paper) | ISBN 9781512428414 (eb pdf)
Subjects: LCSH: African Americans—Civil rights—Georgia—History—20th century—Juvenile literature. | African American girls—Georgia—History—20th century—Juvenile literature. | African American prisoners—Georgia—Social conditions—20th century—Juvenile literature. | African American civil rights workers—Georgia—Juvenile literature. | Civil rights demonstrations—Georgia—Americus—Juvenile literature. | Civil rights movements—Georgia—Juvenile literature. | Prisons—Georgia—Leesburg (Lee County)—Juvenile literature. | Leesburg (Lee County, Ga.)—History—20th century—Juvenile literature.
Classification: LCC E185.61 .S357 2017 (print) | LCC E185.61 (ebook) | DDC 323.1196/07307580904—dc23

LC record available at https://lccn.loc.gov/2016036953

Manufactured in the United States of America
1-37951-19625-3/31/2017

CONTENTS

PROLOGUE

Many young people participated in the Civil Rights Movement. These teenage activists took part in a demonstration called the Children's March in Birmingham, Alabama, in 1963.

In the summer of 1963, record numbers of young Civil Rights activists were arrested for demonstrating in Americus, Georgia. About thirty African American girls were detained in an abandoned stockade outside of town. While the girls lived without medical care, proper food, or working bathroom facilities, their parents didn't even know where they were. Some wouldn't be released for two months. The youngest was eleven years old. The oldest was only sixteen. All stood by their decision to join the Civil Rights Movement.

THIS IS THEIR STORY.

Eleven-year-old Lorena Barnum felt a growing sense of horror as she took in her surroundings.

Her jail cell wasn't large—only about 40 feet (12 meters) long and 15 feet (4.6 m) wide, about the size of a typical classroom. But it was packed with more than thirty girls, who had to live, eat, sleep, and go to the bathroom there. Some of them were her classmates. Some were family. They were all around her age, though she was the youngest.

"The floor was covered with a thin layer of sandy dirt and dust. . . . The walls were damp and felt slimy. . . . The paint on the ceiling was peeling off," Lorena reported afterward.

And it only got worse from there. The cell's single shower was filthy, with ashes stuffed in the drain. There were two toilets, but both were filled to the brim with paper and human waste. There was urine on the floor and feces on old cardboard boxes toward the back. The smell was sickening.

Steel bars secured the broken windows lining the walls. There was no way out.

The girls knew why they were there. This was their punishment for fighting for their rights as American citizens in 1963. And they weren't sorry.

THE GIRLS

CAROL BARNER SEAY
LORENA BARNUM
GLORIA BREEDLOVE
PEARL BROWN
BOBBIE JEAN BUTTS
AGNES CARTER
PATTIE JEAN COLIER
MATTIE CRITTENDEN
BARBARA JEAN DANIELS
GLORIA DEAN
CAROLYN DELOATCH
DIANE DORSEY
JUANITA FREEMAN
ROBERTIENA FREEMAN
HENRIETTA FULLER
SHIRLEY ANN GREEN
VERNA HOLLIS
EVETTE HOSE
MARY FRANCES JACKSON

VYRTIS JACKSON
DOROTHY JONES
EMMA JEAN JONES
  (ALSO KNOWN AS
  EMMA JEAN TIMES)
MELINDA JONES-WILLIAMS
EMMARENE KAIGLER
BARBARA ANN PETERSON
ANNIE LUE RAGANS
JUDITH REID
LAURA RUFF
SANDRA RUSSELL
WILLIE MAE SMITH
ELIZA THOMAS
BILLIE JO THORNTON
LULU M. WESTBROOK
OZELIAR WHITEHEAD
CARRIE MAE WILLIAMS

KEY LOCATIONS

VIRGINIA

TENNESSEE

SOUTH
CAROLINA

Atlanta

Birmingham

GEORGIA

MISSISSIPPI

Montgomery

Americus

Leesburg

Albany

ALABAMA

FLORIDA

0 20 40 60 80 Miles

0   40   80   120 Kilometers

CHAPTER 1

LIFE AS USUAL

In 1963 Juanita Freeman was a regular teenager living in the city of Americus, in Georgia's Sumter County. She sang in her church choir. She joined a dance team. She liked to go to Weston's, a local soda shop, where she could hang out with her friends. But many of her everyday experiences were nothing like what a teenager would expect in twenty-first-century America.

When Juanita went to the local doctor's office, she was required to use the back door instead of the front. It was the same at the Martin Theater, where she had to walk by the Dumpster—picking her way through trash and broken glass scattered on the ground—to get inside. Once there, she was allowed to watch movies from seats in the balcony, but not downstairs.

In the American South, segregation laws kept white citizens separate from African American citizens in both public and private spaces. Facilities for African Americans were often inferior to those for white people. At this bus station in Jackson, Mississippi, pictured in 1961, the waiting room for black people is marked with an Out of Order sign.

Robertiena Freeman, Juanita's sister, was thirteen in 1963. She shares similar memories. When Robertiena shopped for shoes, she had to be fitted in an area set aside for black customers. If a white customer arrived after she did, it didn't matter that she had gotten there first. She would have to wait.

The girls attended one of Americus's two high schools. All the students and teachers were African American. No matter how far they lived from school, black kids walked. White kids rode to their schools in school buses. "You could see injustice all around," Robertiena recalls.

DAILY DISCRIMINATION

The injustices Juanita and Robertiena—and many other teens—experienced each day were all based on racial discrimination. This was a perfectly normal and legal way of life in their hometown, as well as all over the South. Segregation laws, also called Jim Crow laws, required black citizens and white citizens to use separate public facilities or to stay in separate sections of public areas.

Many white people considered themselves superior to African Americans and saw these laws as natural. And black people knew that they could be arrested—or even attacked by white residents—if they crossed the color line.

WHO WAS JIM CROW?

Jim Crow started out as a character created by Thomas Dartmouth Rice, a white singer and dancer in the 1830s and 1840s. Rice performed in blackface, pretending to be a foolish black entertainer named Jim Crow. He traveled throughout the United States and England with his popular act. Other white entertainers even started playing Jim Crow in their own performances.

A few decades later, after slavery was outlawed in the United States, southern states began passing laws and creating a social system that would deny newly freed black citizens their full rights. The name Jim Crow was already associated with making black people look foolish and inferior to whites. So it became a name for the South's segregation laws and customs.

SLAVERY'S LEGACY

Segregation and discrimination in the United States have their roots in the system of slavery. For hundreds of years, millions of African American people were enslaved throughout the nation, mainly in southern states. White people legally owned black people as property and forced these slaves to work for them without pay. This was very profitable for white slave owners. White political leaders defended the practice and passed other laws designed to keep black people under white people's control. And in all aspects of society, white people developed traditions based on racism—the idea that one race is superior to others.

Many activists, both white and black, spoke out against slavery and worked to help enslaved people gain their freedom. The Thirteenth Amendment to the US Constitution eventually outlawed slavery in 1865. The end of legalized slavery didn't mean the end of racism, however. Many white Americans still believed African Americans were an inferior race. They believed they had a right to more power and wealth than black people, and they worked to keep black Americans from succeeding.

After the Civil War ended in 1865, many leaders in southern states passed segregation laws that limited black citizens' opportunities and kept white people in positions of power. These laws touched generations of African American lives.

After slavery was outlawed in the United States, few African American families found good employment opportunities. Many, like these workers in late nineteenth-century Georgia, continued working on large plantations owned by white people. All their pay went toward equipment and rent, so they remained extremely poor.

Some of Americus's young people struck back in their own small ways. When Robertiena went to the movies, she and her friends would sometimes throw popcorn and drinks on the white patrons below. Fourteen-year-old Emma Jean Jones (who also went by the name Emma Jean Times) liked to stir things up at the local Dairy Queen. Instead of ordering on the "colored" side of the counter, she'd march up to the "white" side and insist on service.

"I was bold," she remembers. "My mother said I'd get beat up. She told me I never would have survived slavery days."

After a lot of back and forth with the employees, Emma Jean would eventually get her ice cream. Then she'd say she'd changed her mind and didn't want ice cream after all. It wasn't her way of messing with them. "I was afraid they did something to it," she explains. She didn't want to risk eating food that had been tampered with and that might make her sick.

Despite the risks, Emma Jean couldn't stop herself from challenging her hometown's customs.

"I heard the way [white] people talked to older [black] people my mother's age," she recalls. "I wasn't gonna have it."

CUSTOMS OF DISRESPECT

By challenging the Dairy Queen employees, Emma Jean wasn't simply ignoring the segregation law. She was going against an unwritten code that controlled all aspects of behavior between black Americans and white Americans. Etiquette demanded that black people conduct themselves as a second-class citizen at all times.

In the world Emma Jean grew up in, white people didn't address black people by their names or use titles of respect like Mr., Mrs., and Miss. Black men were called "boy," "uncle," "old man," and "nigger." Black women were called "auntie" or "girl." Black people, on the other hand, had to speak to white people respectfully.

Even if black and white people got along and felt friendly toward each other, they couldn't easily develop an equal relationship. In conversation, black people were not supposed to challenge anything a white person said, even if it was incorrect. Black people knew they were not supposed to show superior knowledge or intelligence.

African Americans also were not allowed to show public affection. Black men were not allowed to touch white women, even to shake hands.

White police officers attack a black man in Harlem, New York, in 1964. Hostile treatment of black Americans occurred in northern states as well as southern states.

If a white person drove a black person someplace, the black passenger was expected to sit in the backseat. At intersections, white drivers always had the right of way.

Defying this etiquette wasn't simply considered bad manners. Everyone knew the possible consequences were very serious. Many white people who believed in segregation were willing to use violence to intimidate and punish black people for breaking the rules. A black person who drank from the "white" water fountain might be beaten up. Black men could be lynched for a slight as minor as looking at a white woman. And African Americans couldn't count on any legal protections against this kind of violence. Police officers, prosecutors, judges, juries, and prison officials were all white and generally didn't go out of their way to ensure black citizens' safety. Few white people who committed crimes against black people faced legal consequences

Questioning and confronting Jim Crow etiquette was as dangerous as breaking the law.

SEGREGATED SOCIETY

The way Lorena Barnum remembers it, black people and white people mainly just kept apart in Americus. "We were so segregated. There was little interaction with white people," she recalls.

Lorena's memories include shopping at the nicest dress shop in town, where she wasn't allowed to try on clothes in the dressing room. She saw the way her mother shopped for hats without the opportunity to try them on. She went to restaurants where she and her family couldn't sit down but had to order

THE KKK

The Ku Klux Klan, or KKK, was a citizens' group founded by a group of white ex-Confederate soldiers in the South in 1866. Members believed that white people were superior to black people. The group opposed any policies that would help newly freed black Americans. Nearly a century later, the organization was still a powerful force of racial hatred in the South. Members regularly took part in violent acts against black people and white Civil Rights supporters. When KKK members carried out bombings, lynchings (killings, usually hangings), shootings, and beatings, they hid their identities by wearing hooded white robes.

Members of the Ku Klux Klan, wearing the group's distinctive white gowns and hoods, lead new members (in face masks) at a gathering in Atlanta, Georgia.

takeout at a side window. And she always shrank from using the filthy public bathrooms designated for black people.

"I remember being small, saying, 'I don't want to go in there,'" she says.

Everywhere she looked, she noticed the contrasts—like how Kress's, the five-and-dime store, had a fancy refrigerated water fountain for white people and a little basin with a spigot for black people. But for a long time, she didn't ask why. It was just the way things were.

LAWS OF THE LAND

Segregation laws touched every area of people's lives. These were some of Georgia's laws during the 1960s:

BARBERS

No colored barber shall serve as a barber to white women or girls.

AMATEUR BASEBALL

It shall be unlawful for any amateur white baseball team to play baseball on any vacant lot or baseball diamond within two blocks of a playground devoted to the Negro race, and it shall be unlawful for any amateur colored baseball team to play baseball in any vacant lot or baseball diamond within two blocks of any playground devoted to the white race.

BURIAL

The officer in charge shall not bury, or allow to be buried, any colored persons upon ground set apart or used for the burial of white persons.

INTERMARRIAGE

It shall be unlawful for a white person to marry anyone except a white person. Any marriage in violation of this section shall be void.

MENTAL HOSPITALS

The Board of Control shall see that proper and distinct apartments are arranged for said patients, so that in no case shall Negroes and white persons be together.

PARKS

It shall be unlawful for colored people to frequent any park owned or maintained by the city for the benefit, use and enjoyment of white persons . . . and unlawful for any white person to frequent any park owned or maintained by the city for the use and benefit of colored persons.

RESTAURANTS

All persons licensed to conduct a restaurant shall serve either white people exclusively or colored people exclusively and shall not sell to the two races within the same room or serve the two races anywhere under the same license.

As she got older, though, Lorena started to take segregation more personally.

She realized that black businesses, schools, and other facilities had far less money and fewer resources than those of white people. Her mother was a science teacher and a basketball coach at the local black high school. Lorena remembers the team practiced on dirt because the school had no gym.

Schools for black students lacked the money to buy as many supplies as schools for white students. The children pictured here, in a New Orleans, Louisiana, classroom in 1954, would have had limited access to up-to-date textbooks, science lab equipment, and other necessary tools.

She remembers her mother had two microscopes for all of her students, and she raised money to buy her own supplies. "I knew as a teacher's daughter how rare it was for students to have what they needed," she says. "It was such a big topic in our household."

Juanita has similar memories of the local black school. Her desk was old and scratched. Her textbooks were outdated, with the names of former students who'd used them listed in the front. She might get a chance to do science lab work only once or twice during the whole school year—if the teacher could raise money or afford to spend her own money to buy test tubes and other equipment.

Twelve-year-old Lulu Westbrook also saw how segregation fed racial inequality in Americus. Dentists didn't want to treat her. She was turned away from the public library. Workers at the Health Department took one look at her dark skin and refused to use a fresh needle for her shots.

Lulu resented how this unequal treatment held her back. And she knew that if something didn't change, she would keep running into limitations based on the color of her skin. Like many black teens growing up in the 1960s, she wondered: What would happen after she graduated from high school? Where would she go from here?

When Carolyn DeLoatch was growing up in Americus, her father had a stable job as a school principal. She didn't understand at the time why other kids spent summers picking cotton and peaches with their families. But since her friends were going to the fields, she wanted to try it too. She begged her parents, and they finally allowed it when she was fourteen.

"I thought it would be fun. Everyone was going," she recalls.

Carolyn only picked cotton a couple of times, but she vividly remembers the days she spent working in the fields for her white employers.

African American workers pick cotton in Louisiana in the 1940s. In the twentieth century, like the previous century, African Americans struggled to find fair-paying jobs.

"They weren't nice to us. The way they talked to [us] was kind of rough," she says. "It was hot, grueling. The work was hard. The day was long. It was awful. I learned that I did not want to do that and that it was not fun."

But the work wasn't optional for everyone. Lulu Westbrook recalls picking cotton and peaches in the Georgia heat when she was ten, eleven, and twelve years old. Some days, the temperature rose to 100°F (38°C). No matter how brutal the weather was, she worked all day long.

"That was how we made our living," she recalls.

And that was how *many* black families had to earn a living in the early 1960s—juggling several low-paying jobs working for white employers. In the South, the job market was segregated just like every other aspect of society. Jobs with power, status, and a good salary almost always went to white applicants. Most black citizens—even college graduates—worked in manual labor or service positions. This work was often physically taxing and typically paid less than other kinds of jobs.

By 1963 a new generation of young black Americans was beginning to recognize the shadow that segregation cast over their futures. How could they hope to do better than their parents? Too many opportunities were closed to them, even if they got a college education. Lulu's older brother, James, attended Fort Valley State University, in Fort Valley, Georgia. But no good jobs were

EARNING POTENTIAL

The average income for US families in 1960 was $5,600. Data from the 1960 US census shows many more black families than white families lived on less.

STATE	% OF WHITE FAMILIES EARNING LESS THAN $4,000[1]	% NONWHITE FAMILIES EARNING LESS THAN $4,000
Georgia	24.1	78.7
Kentucky	33.6	66.3
Louisiana	22.7	75.2
Mississippi	33.3	88
Tennessee	32	72.4

[1] Income of $4,000 in 1960 is equivalent to about $32,000 in 2016.

available for black college graduates. The adults Lulu knew, including her own parents, worked for white people. They didn't earn nearly enough, and white people didn't treat them respectfully either. "No matter how educated you were, you were still a nigger to some of them," she says.

TAKING ACTION

Black people needed new laws to protect them from discrimination. But they couldn't even elect officials who might change the laws and protect their rights. Preventing black people from exercising their right to vote was standard practice throughout the South. In several states, citizens had to pay a poll tax that poor black people couldn't afford. In even more states, including Georgia, black people had to pass impossibly complicated literacy tests and be judged morally fit to vote by a white registrar. Some lost their jobs and homes for even trying to register. Others were arrested by local authorities or even lynched by white citizens.

In 1963, 25,000 people lived in Sumter County, Georgia. Of these, 52 percent—more than 14,000 people—were black. Yet only 300 black voters were registered. Other southern communities had even fewer registered black voters. About 8,000 black people lived in Pike County, Mississippi, in the early 1960s. Only 200 were registered to vote in 1961. Walthall County, Mississippi, had 3,000 black residents and no black voters that year.

Like other black Americans, Lulu was tired of waiting for racist attitudes to change. All across the country, people had started taking action instead. They

WHITE SUPPORT FOR CIVIL RIGHTS

While most Civil Rights activists were black southerners, the Movement also had many other supporters, including white southerners. In Georgia some of those white supporters were members of Sumter County's Koinonia Farm, where black and white people had lived and farmed together since 1942. Koinonians were Christians who believed in treating all people with dignity, justice, and love. Their values mirrored the philosophy that drove the Civil Rights Movement. During the 1950s and 1960s, white citizens harassed and threatened the Koinonians and nearly destroyed their farm. The community survived and continues to work toward racial equality and social justice.

Sit-ins at segregated lunch counters became a powerfully symbolic tactic for Civil Rights demonstrators. These young activists sit at a "whites only" lunch counter in Greensborough, North Carolina, in 1960.

spoke out against segregation and other forms of racial discrimination and demanded equal rights in their communities. These actions were part of the Civil Rights Movement, an American crusade for racial equality.

The Civil Rights Movement had started gaining momentum in 1954. Activists were committed to ending racial discrimination through peaceful methods. They took only nonviolent action, such as marching in demonstrations. Black activists often broke segregation laws. Freedom Rides on segregated cross-country buses and sit-ins at segregated facilities were common tactics for peaceful protesters. When police responded with violent methods to end their protests, activists often simply sat down or began praying. They refused to fight, even to defend themselves.

In 1961 the Movement came to Albany, Georgia, a city close to Americus. The city had caught the attention of the Student Nonviolent Coordinating Committee (SNCC, pronounced "snick"), an organization of young activists. SNCC members led rallies, demonstrations, and a voter registration drive for the city's black citizens. The Movement captured national attention when hundreds of protesters, including one of its prominent leaders, the Reverend Dr. Martin Luther King Jr., were jailed in Albany.

"One of the sad facts in this situation is that while there are more than 20,000 Negroes in Albany's 58,000 population, the Negroes obviously have had little to say about the government and policing of the city," read an August 1962 editorial in the *New York Times*. "History and custom had already made the situation a racial one before Dr. King moved in with his doctrine of peaceful protest."

About 40 miles (64 kilometers) north, Americus was a smaller city experiencing similar problems. SNCC wanted to help Americus challenge this way of life by registering black voters and protesting Jim Crow laws. Workers met with local black leaders. The Reverend J. R. Campbell, the Reverend R. L. Freeman, and Mabel Barnum (owner of Barnum Funeral Home) became leaders of the Movement. They organized mass meetings at local churches, as well as at Barnum Funeral Home.

Mass meetings made it easy for people to come together and get involved in the cause. For some, though, it would have been impossible to not get involved. Juanita and Robertiena were Freeman's daughters. Lorena remembers attending meetings and making posters at Barnum Funeral Home, her grandmother Mabel's business. She remembers that when protesters were arrested, her father helped get them released from jail.

"Out-of-towners, SNCC mostly, would stay with us for weeks and months at a time to come and work in the community," Lorena recalls. "[The Movement] was all-consuming in my household. It was a unique time."

For those who didn't have parents or other adult relatives involved in the Movement, mass meetings were a place to learn about what was happening. Lulu attended meetings with her brothers, sister, and niece. She remembers how eager she was to hear what the leaders had to say about the Movement's mission across the South. "[Martin Luther] King's word spread like wildfire," she recalls. "We thought, 'Let's try to change *our* town.'"

THE MOVEMENT IN AMERICUS

The black residents of Americus did just that. At mass meetings, they planned protests, including marches and sit-ins. They heard moving speeches and sang freedom songs. When they lifted up their voices together, they were empowered to go out and do what needed to be done—despite the very real dangers they faced.

SNCC

In 1960 Ella Baker, director of the Southern Christian Leadership Conference, saw a need for a separate organization for younger Civil Rights activists. She helped create the Student Nonviolent Coordinating Committee, which would give black college students opportunities to "channel their energy and dedication" to the Movement. It was also integrated, meaning many white students from all over the country got involved with the organization too.

The students planned demonstrations that were considered radical by other Civil Rights organizations. They held voter registration drives and played a major role in the Freedom Rides of 1961, desegregating cross-country buses on long, dangerous trips. They were willing to take big chances for their cause by publicly defying the laws and customs of segregation.

Activist Ella Baker ran the Southern Christian Leadership Conference from 1957 to 1960. She then ran SNCC from 1960 to 1962.

Segregationists often attacked buses carrying Freedom Riders. A fire bomb destroyed this bus in 1961.

Though the Movement had a large base of supporters, it also faced powerful opposition. Across the country, about 55 percent of Americans supported equal rights legislation. But the other 45 percent included many white law enforcement officials, politicians, and ordinary citizens determined to suppress the Movement's aims. When Civil Rights activists participated in peaceful demonstrations, they could expect a violent reaction from local police. Officers might beat them, order vicious police dogs to attack them, or blast them with water from powerful fire hoses. No matter what happened, though, the protesters were instructed not to fight back.

"We were trained how to protect ourselves if we was hit over the head. Go to the ground. Sometimes we would kneel and pray," Lulu recalls. "We knew at some point we would be taken to jail."

Even knowing the risks, Carolyn DeLoatch decided to get involved. But her parents didn't want her or her brother to participate in the Movement's activities. At first, Carolyn respected their wishes. After all, they'd always made certain that she didn't feel unsafe or disrespected in her hometown. "My parents did a really good job of shielding us from [racism]," she recalls. Yet during the summer of 1963, fifteen-year-old Carolyn started becoming more aware of injustices she hadn't paid attention to before. She was drawn into the activism all around her.

BIG SIX LEADERS

Several organizations worked together to build the Civil Rights Movement. Founders of those organizations became known as the Big Six leaders of the Movement:

- James Farmer, national director of the Congress of Racial Equality (CORE)
- James Forman, executive secretary of the Student Nonviolent Coordinating Committee (SNCC)
- Martin Luther King, president of the Southern Christian Leadership Conference (SCLC)
- A. Philip Randolph, president of the Brotherhood of Sleeping Car Porters
- Roy Wilkins, executive secretary of the National Association for the Advancement of Colored People (NAACP)
- Whitney Young Jr., executive director of the National Urban League

Police in Birmingham, Alabama, spray Civil Rights demonstrators with high-pressure water from fire hoses. The powerful blasts of water could severely injure people.

"Some friends had been to a mass meeting and invited me to go. I listened and was immediately enthralled," she says. "They were talking about African American people and how we were not free. I understood and related and wanted to be a part of it."

First, however, she had long talks with her parents about what could happen if she took a public stand for equal rights. Besides being sent to jail herself, Carolyn would also be putting her parents in a terrible position. If their daughter became a Civil Rights activist, they could be fired.

"A lot of older people were scared of losing their jobs," Juanita says. "Fifty percent of employment was in a white person's kitchen or restaurant. White person would tell them, 'You'd better not march.'"

The threat kept many adults out of the Movement. And it was a powerful motivator meant to keep their kids away too.

But it wasn't powerful enough.

CHAPTER 3
UNDER ARREST!

Black Americans who got involved in the Civil Rights Movement had a lot to gain. They hoped to win the freedom from the restrictions and the disrespect they'd been forced to endure all their lives. They hoped to gain an equal voice in their communities and in their government. They hoped to secure opportunities for themselves as well as for future generations of their families.

But they had a lot to lose too. Adults especially were on shaky ground. If they were jailed, they would lose work time as well as pay. Whether they were jailed or not, they could lose their jobs altogether if an employer didn't approve of their activities. Many black American adults simply couldn't afford to take that risk.

Schoolchildren in Birmingham, Alabama, head to jail in May 1963, after participating in a Civil Rights protest.

Many children and teens felt compelled to take the risk—even if their involvement called attention to their families. "We all wanted change," Lulu remembers. "We wanted better schools. We wanted better jobs. We wanted to be treated equally. It was a matter of standing up for what you knew was right."

Going to jail wasn't just a side effect of Civil Rights activism. It was one of the main tactics protesters used to call attention to their cause. Activists focused on filling the jails so authorities would see that the Movement couldn't be stopped. And all across the country, children were taking part in this risky but effective strategy.

In May 1963, thousands of children in Birmingham, Alabama, took part in the Children's March, a series of nonviolent Civil Rights demonstrations. Some protesters were as young as six years old. Many were beaten by police, attacked by police dogs, sprayed with fire hoses, and arrested. Their bravery called national attention to the Movement.

Children and teens were taking brave steps in Americus too. Once school let out in June 1963, they had time to march and demonstrate. And that meant being carted off to jail. Local law enforcement, led by Americus police chief Ross Chambliss and Sumter County sheriff Fred Chappell, didn't hesitate to arrest Civil Rights activists, including children and teens. Chappell was a known racist who had arrested Martin Luther King in 1961. King is said to have described him as "the meanest man in the world."

Lulu was arrested while marching toward the Martin Theater. She and other young people sang freedom songs and carried signs that spoke for them. "We were very peaceful. We had been trained. We had to take an oath of nonviolence," Lulu remembers. "The cops were the ones that had sticks and dogs and billy clubs."

The Americus police force was not unusual for arresting Civil Rights activists. According to the US Justice Department, during the first half of 1963, more than

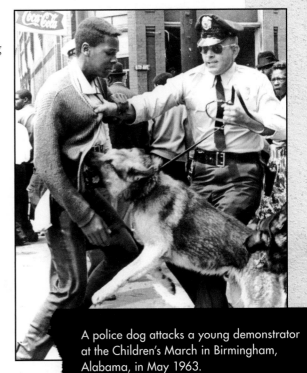

A police dog attacks a young demonstrator at the Children's March in Birmingham, Alabama, in May 1963.

978 Civil Rights demonstrations took place in 109 American cities. Thousands of activists were arrested. Still, Americus stood out for its high number of arrests of young people during the summer of 1963.

"That summer, little by little, the population of young people was populating the jails," Lorena Barnum, then eleven, recalls.

As older teens were arrested, younger teens and children stepped up their activism. Lorena knew demonstrating could be dangerous. Her brother had tried to integrate the city's Martin Theater so that black patrons could use the front door and sit downstairs like white patrons. Police sprayed demonstrators with powerful fire hoses and sicced their dogs on them.

Lorena didn't let her brother's experience scare her away from the Movement. Late that summer, Lorena went to the middle school to protest, on behalf of all the kids who were still in jail. She and the other demonstrators had a specific demand. They wanted those young people released from jail by the time school started. It seemed a reasonable request. But soon enough, the demonstrators were in a paddy wagon themselves.

Lorena was on her way to jail.

KNOWN RISKS

It was August 1963, and Americus kids kept winding up in jail. But this didn't surprise anyone. Young people joined the protests knowing full well they'd be arrested. They were ready.

JUVENILES' RIGHTS

Georgia's Department of Juvenile Justice protects the legal rights of people under the age of seventeen when they are arrested and taken into custody. The department bans bullying, harassment, and discrimination. It requires that youth be allowed to make and receive phone calls.

The department also sets standards for basic quality of life necessities. Young people in custody must be allowed to eat and sleep without interference. They must be allowed to maintain their physical, mental, and emotional health through regular exercise. They must have access to medical care and functioning bathroom facilities.

The Department of Juvenile Justice wasn't around to protect the legal rights of 1960s Civil Rights protesters. It was created in 1992.

Carolyn DeLoatch waited to join a protest until her father—who traveled for his work—was back in town. That way, her mother wouldn't be alone for long. On the day of the protest, Carolyn took her brother with her.

"We left knowing we would go to jail that day," she says.

Emma Jean demonstrated at Staley High School. "I wasn't really surprised I got arrested. Most kids were getting arrested," she recalls. "I wasn't really scared."

Civil Rights demonstrators in Nashville, Tennessee, cram into a police paddy wagon in 1964.

Barbara Jean Daniels remembers protesting at the Martin Theater and other spots in town during the summer of 1963, the year she was fourteen. She also remembers being taken to jail more than once. "Every time we went uptown, they were locking our butts up," she says.

Robertiena Freeman recalls police officers pushing her into a paddy wagon after she protested downtown. She and her fellow demonstrators were taken to the city jail, where police put some of them in a sweatbox—a tiny compartment used for solitary confinement. "It was very hot and dark," she says.

Lorena Barnum remembers spending the night in the city jail. "There was one big cell [or] room. There must have been 20 of us or more," she recalls. "We put the mattresses in the middle of the floor so everyone could sleep and pushed the beds back."

Many young protesters spent at least one night under arrest in town. The accommodations at the Americus city jail weren't comfortable. The kids weren't treated kindly. But the surroundings were familiar. Conditions were bearable and somewhat predictable.

Then one morning, police started moving some of the girls to another location outside Americus.

"They put us in a paddy wagon," Emma Jean remembers. "They loaded us out like animals. We couldn't see out. We didn't know where we were going."

Even after they reached their destination—a facility 24 miles (39 km) away in Leesburg—they couldn't be sure where they were. All they knew was their situation had gone from bad to worse.

When the paddy wagon stopped, police officers roughly unloaded the girls and herded them into a long concrete room. The floor and walls were filthy. The room was littered with debris. Green paint peeled from the ceiling. Bars crossed eight or ten broken-out windows. Water dripped continuously from a showerhead toward the back.

About twenty iron beds were set up for the girls to use—not that they wanted to. "The mattresses were sandy and gritty and so dirty you could see it just by looking at it," reported Robertiena Freeman, who was brought to the stockade on August 21, 1963. "And some were so ripped the cotton was coming out of them."

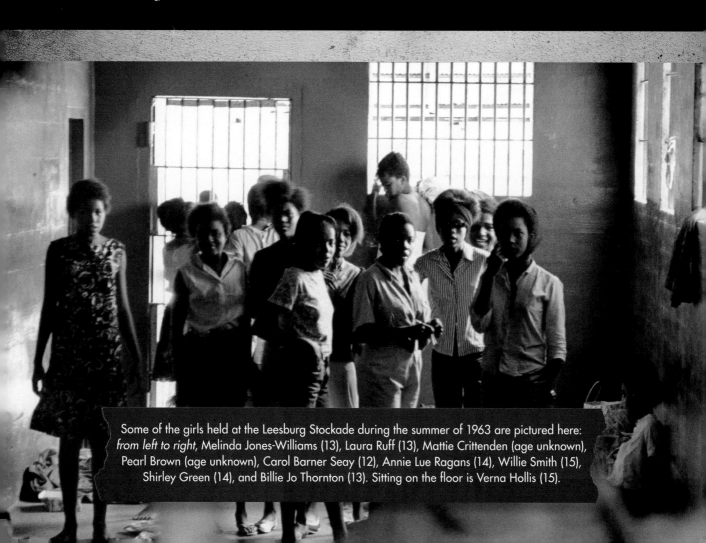

Some of the girls held at the Leesburg Stockade during the summer of 1963 are pictured here: *from left to right*, Melinda Jones-Williams (13), Laura Ruff (13), Mattie Crittenden (age unknown), Pearl Brown (age unknown), Carol Barner Seay (12), Annie Lue Ragans (14), Willie Smith (15), Shirley Green (14), and Billie Jo Thornton (13). Sitting on the floor is Verna Hollis (15).

HOW MANY GIRLS WERE AT LEESBURG?

A list compiled by the Albany Civil Rights Institute at Old Mt. Zion, in Albany, Georgia, includes the names of thirty-three Americus girls who were prisoners at Leesburg Stockade. But historical evidence indicates other young girls from Americus were jailed there too. A photo of Americus girls held at Leesburg Stockade names Carol Broner, Janet Broner, Linda Brown, Mattie Criton, Goldie Mae Harris, Eliza Thomas, Sandra Thornton, and Zelda Whitehead. Some of these names are misspellings of known girls' names, while others may identify additional girls. Many girls, including Emma Jean, spoke about their experiences afterward and signed written affidavits. (Emma Jean's last name is recorded as Times, her father's last name. She also went by her mother's maiden name, Jones.) A girl named Melinda Jones-Williams was later identified by another former prisoner. The Leesburg Stockade may have held even more Americus girls who've never been identified or come forward to tell their story.

None of the girls knew it, but officials had taken them to Leesburg Stockade, in Lee County, Georgia. The building was an old prison that had been built during the Civil War era and eventually abandoned.

The girls were far from home. They were prisoners in a place where they could plainly see that even their basic human need for cleanliness wouldn't be respected.

"It looked as though life hadn't been there in ten years it was so dusty," one girl, Eliza Thomas, reported. "The walls were dirty also; everything was dirty."

By some accounts, Leesburg Stockade had, in fact, been used to house other young female prisoners a year or two before. Sam Mahone, an Americus Civil Rights activist, recalls that girls from Albany, Georgia, were sent to Leesburg Stockade too. But Eliza may have been right in guessing the cell hadn't been used—or at least cleaned—in recent years.

Law enforcement officials had to know Leesburg Stockade was unsafe and unsanitary, but that didn't stop them from locking up their young prisoners from Americus there. An old white man the girls called Pops acted as a guard. According to varying reports, there were other guards as well.

ON THEIR OWN

The thirty or so Americus girls locked up at Leesburg Stockade in 1963 didn't arrive—or leave—all at once. They were brought in at different times between August and September. Some were released within just a few days. Others spent weeks there. The longest stay is reported to be about two months.

Word got out that the girls were being held at the Leesburg Stockade, but there wasn't much anyone could do about it. For the most part, neither the girls' families nor the local Movement activists were even allowed to visit the prisoners. Emma Jean remembers one girl's mother bringing the girls a box of food that they all shared. Barbara Jean Daniels remembers using sanitary napkins donated by people who attended the Movement's mass meetings. But girls were mainly forced to fend for themselves.

They did the best they could to meet their basic needs. The cell wasn't designed for that many people to sleep, wash, and use the bathroom for as long as they were held there. One report from 1963 says the cell was actually built to hold only four prisoners.

TYPICALLY HORRIFIC

Conditions at the Leesburg Stockade were undoubtedly horrific. In many ways, however, they were typical of what Civil Rights activists experienced when they were arrested and jails became overcrowded. At the same time the girls were taken to Leesburg, their male friends, also teenagers, were taken to a facility in Dawson, Georgia, about 30 miles (48 km) from Americus. They lived in similar conditions.

Back in Americus, eighteen-year-old Lena Turner, who was held at the city jail for fifty-two days beginning in the late summer of 1963, faced an equally appalling situation. "The sink was clogged and filled with dirty water. The commode was clogged with waste. The mattresses were filthy and infested with bedbugs and roaches," she reported in an affidavit afterward.

Lorine Sanders, another young woman who was at the jail during the same time as Lena, said, "In my cell there were dirty mattresses. We asked for soap but was refused. There was no hot water in the cell. We used a nasty wash basin to wash our face and hands. The ventilation was poor and the place was hot all the time."

To create a sleeping area, the girls did their best with only thin, dirty mattresses and a few wool blankets to share. The area was crowded and uncomfortable because they couldn't use all the mattresses. "Some of the mattresses were so bad some of the girls were afraid to sleep on them," Robertiena said. "So we picked out the ones we thought we could sleep on and pushed them to the front. "We put the bad ones, which had bugs crawling over them, to the back."

The only food the guards provided for the girls was cold, greasy, partially cooked hamburgers. The hamburgers were delivered once a day—usually around eleven in the morning but sometimes as late as three in the afternoon—and the girls got four each.

As for drinks, the guards didn't offer the girls anything to quench their thirst during the sweltering summer days. The girls could only get water from the shower, catching it in two or three tin cups they were given to share. The water was almost as bad as the food: warm or hot, sometimes cloudy, and tasting of rust. But they didn't have the luxury of turning it down. There was nothing else to drink, and without water, they wouldn't survive.

The worst thing about the cell was the bathroom facilities. "There were two toilets and they were stopped up when I got there," Robertiena reported. "They wouldn't work."

This showerhead was the girls' only available source of water in the stockade.

With no way out and no one willing to fix the facilities, the girls had limited options. At first, the girls kept using the toilets anyway—until they began overflowing. Then they were forced to urinate in the shower or on sections of the floor. When they needed to move their bowels, many girls resorted to using the discarded mattresses in the back of the room. Some just didn't go at all. One girl reported waiting out the entire nine and a half days she was imprisoned. Another was reportedly constipated for sixteen days. Long-term constipation is a serious issue that can lead to intense pain, vomiting, and impaction—a condition that requires medical attention.

The dripping shower worked well enough to keep the girls clean—at least in the beginning. Emma Jean later reported that she used it once and that some kids showered every day while she was there. Very soon, though, it became dirty from being used as a makeshift toilet. Sanitary napkins and wastepaper littered the shower floor. The smell of unwashed bodies in the sweltering Georgia heat mingled horribly with the odor of the waste materials collecting in the cell. "The stench was awful," remembers Juanita Freeman. "You had to go to the windows to get fresh air." With temperatures hovering above 90°F (32°C) throughout August, the outside air offered little relief for the girls.

COURAGE PREVAILS

Despite the girls' discomfort and fear, the mood in the cell was hopeful. The girls sang freedom songs and prayed together. They joked and did one another's hair to pass the long, hot days. On the outside, they weren't all close friends. They came from different backgrounds. Some had grown up in comfortable

THE AMERICUS FOUR

Americus became known nationwide when the media learned about the Americus Four, adult male activists who were arrested after a protest that ended in police brutality.

The protest began when about two hundred marchers made their way through a black neighborhood on August 8. Police tried to stop them by firing shots into the air. When that didn't work, they beat the activists with clubs, used an electric cattle prod on at least one, and shot a black man for walking through a white neighborhood.

SNCC workers Don Harris, John Perdew, and Ralph Allen, and CORE activist Zev Aelony were arrested for their involvement and charged under Georgia's 1871 Anti-Treason Act. If convicted, they could be executed. Meanwhile, they could be held in jail without bail for months.

As word got out about their situation, they became known as the Americus Four. In November, more than three months after their arrest, the charges were dropped and they were finally released.

houses, others in shotgun shacks. But in jail, those differences didn't matter. They were all Civil Rights activists, fighting together for a common cause.

The way Carolyn DeLoatch remembers it, they were jubilant in their overcrowded cell. By demonstrating, getting arrested, and enduring the hardships of their time in jail, the girls knew they'd taken a strong stand for a cause that meant so much to them.

"We were willing to die for it," recalls Juanita Freeman. "That took the fear out of you. I think everyone who went to jail was willing to die."

CHAPTER 5
DOING TIME

Snake!" someone screamed. "Snake!"

Near panic broke out when the girls spotted a diamondback rattlesnake trapped in their cell with them. No one could be sure how it got in there. Did it slither in through a crack in the floor? Did the guard toss it in to scare them?

Even if he had, there was no one else to call for, no one else who might help. "Snake!" they screamed.

But no one came.

Two girls try to get some rest on the floor of the stockade.

The girls tried to hit the snake with brooms, pieces from broken bed frames, and anything else they could find. Finally, after about thirty minutes, the guard opened the cell door. The way some remember it, he let the girls run outside while he killed the snake.

Dancing in the fresh air, the girls lapped up their freedom. But trying to escape seemed out of the question. For one thing, they had no idea where they were or how they could get home. Besides that, a scarier thought occurred to some of them. An escape attempt might be exactly what the guard wanted. If they ran, he'd have an excuse to shoot them.

"We thought it wise to go back inside and shut the door," Juanita Freeman recalls.

The incident with the snake was a breaking point, though. The girls were outraged they'd had to wait so long for help. And they were fed up with every indignity they were suffering—the lack of toilet facilities, toilet paper, and sanitary napkins; the sickening food; the filth and odor; the leering looks from the guard when they tried to wash their clothes and had to wait in their underthings for them to dry.

ACTIVISTS TAKE ACTION

The girls took matters into their own hands, setting fire to the mattresses they'd been forced to use for bowel movements.

"We burned them to get rid of the feces and the awful odor. We felt this was the only way to get rid of them. The smoke also helped to get rid of the mosquitos," Robertiena Freeman reported later. The girls knew their act of defiance was risky. The guards might use it as an excuse to punish them. "That night the girls were afraid to sleep too far up front, and so in some beds there were as many as six of us."

The girls' jailers quickly penalized them for their defiant independence. "The very next day the guards took away our remaining beds because we were singing and praying," Robertiena said. "So then we started sleeping on the floor with no mattresses, no beds, no blankets, no sheets, no nothing. The floor was wet with waste material from when they [the guards] had been dragging the mattresses out of the cell."

New girls who arrived at Leesburg Stockade found there was no furniture in the cell at all. "The floor was cold," thirteen-year-old Henrietta Fuller reported.

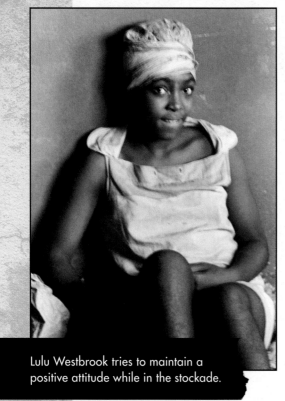

Lulu Westbrook tries to maintain a positive attitude while in the stockade.

"You lay down for a while and soon it starts hurting you so you sit up for a while and it starts hurting so you have to walk around for a while."

At night, the girls had to rest on the cold, dirty, concrete floor. Even if they managed to get some sleep, they woke with cramps in their backs each morning.

After a few nights with only their clothes to cover them, the girls got back some of their smelly, burned blankets. But then the guards decided not to turn on the overhead light at night. Without any light, it was impossible to see in the cell after sundown. "Before they dragged out the beds we had lights, but after that we had them no more," Robertiena reported. "You had to stay put all night because it was too dark to walk, and one girl had cut her head when lights were out earlier in my stay there."

Another problem was bugs, which easily made their way in through the broken windows. Flies, gnats, and mosquitoes were drawn to the waste materials collecting in the cell. The girls couldn't escape them when they flew directly from the waste onto their bare arms and legs. One night Eliza Thomas pulled a cockroach from her hair.

MORE MISTREATMENT

By the time Lorena Barnum arrived at Leesburg, on August 31, 1963, some of the girls had been there for weeks. Did their families even know where they were? Would they ever be released?

The way most remember it, they had no contact with the outside world. All they could do was sing and pray, do one another's hair, play cards . . . and wait.

For her own sake, Lorena was relieved to see a few familiar faces among the girls sharing her cell. Her cousin, Billie Jo Thornton, was there, and it was comforting to be with family. "Of course I was scared, but I was with people I knew. It was kind of an adventure," she recalls. "As a kid, it's laughing and fun until night comes and you want your mama."

Even with a positive outlook, there was no denying the situation was bad. Lorena was horrified by the living conditions in the cell. She held her nose, but the smell was so bad she felt sick to her stomach.

As for the food: "I wouldn't feed it to my pets."

WORDS OF HOPE

Carolyn DeLoatch got so sick at Leesburg Stockade that she was taken back to the Americus city jail, where a doctor could treat her. "The food was just horrible. I couldn't keep it down," she recalls. "I had some stomach thing."

As she remembers it, she was at the Americus jail on August 28, 1963. And the guards had their TV on. They were watching a momentous event taking place in Washington, DC.

From her jail cell, Carolyn listened to a broadcast of the March on Washington. Thousands of Civil Rights supporters had gathered on Washington, DC's National Mall, near the Washington Monument, to demand equal rights. She heard Martin Luther King tell the world about his dream of racial equality for all Americans. It was a dream shared by every Civil Rights activist in the country—including the young girls from Americus, Georgia, who were suffering in hopes of making that dream come true.

Thousands of Civil Rights supporters demonstrated at the March on Washington in August 1963.

One Big Six leader was missing from the March on Washington: James Farmer, a founder of the Congress of Racial Equality (CORE). Like the girls at Leesburg Stockade, he was imprisoned at the time for his Civil Rights activities. Charged with disturbing the peace, Farmer was being held in a Louisiana jail.

Farmer sent a speech to be read by another activist at the March on Washington. It included these words:

> *We are fighting not only for our rights and our freedom; we are fighting not only to make our nation safe for the democracy it preaches. We are fighting also to give our old world a fighting chance for survival. We are fighting to give millions of babies yet unborn—black, white, red, yellow and brown—a chance to see day and to carry on the battle to remove the night of hate, hunger and disease from the world. . . . You, thus, are at the center of the world's stage. Play well your roles in your struggle for freedom on the thousands of communities from which you come throughout the land. Act with valor and with dignity, and without fear.*

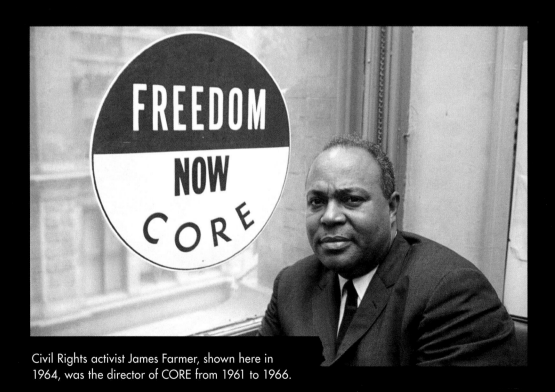

Civil Rights activist James Farmer, shown here in 1964, was the director of CORE from 1961 to 1966.

SUFFERING AND SICK

After spending a night in the Americus city jail, Carolyn felt better. Authorities took her straight back to the Leesburg Stockade. She was lucky she'd seen a doctor at all. Most girls who developed health problems at Leesburg were ignored. And there was certainly no shortage of ailments. Eliza Thomas's skin started breaking out. Between her toes, the skin began to peel. "Some girls got athlete's foot," reported Emma Jean. "One girl had a weak heart and got pains in her chest when she was there. Another girl had sinus trouble and had an asthma attack in jail. All these girls asked for a doctor but the Leesburg Stockade didn't have one."

Lorena Barnum remembers a particularly scary experience. "One late evening two of the girls were sick. One girl had a bad heart and the other a bad appendix. One girl was trembling so bad and the other was crying and asking for help so we called for the guard. He ignored us for about 15 minutes and when he came, he said that he wouldn't come again until [the other guard returned]. We called again and after several hours [another] man came. He said there was nothing wrong with the girls. He said, 'If they aren't dead by morning, we'll come and look at them again.'"

Perhaps by sheer luck, both girls felt better by morning.

CHAPTER 6
POWER IN PICTURES

The girls in Leesburg Stockade had no way of knowing that one student activist from Chicago might change everything for them. Danny Lyon had gotten involved with the Movement long before the girls were jailed. Since then he'd become a full-time SNCC worker armed with a powerful and peaceful weapon: a camera.

In 1962 Danny Lyon was a twenty-year-old college student at the University of Chicago. One day, Danny noticed a photograph in the student newspaper. It showed a young white man being clubbed by police for his involvement in a Civil Rights protest down south. The man was Tom Hayden, a student from the University of Michigan at Ann Arbor.

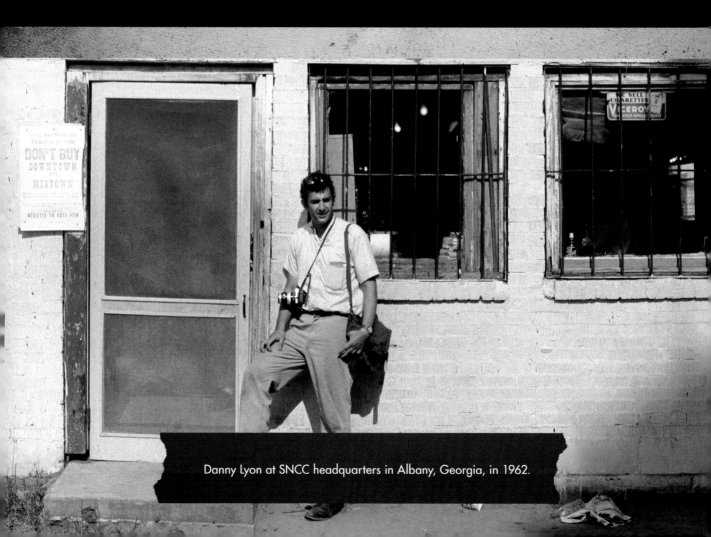

Danny Lyon at SNCC headquarters in Albany, Georgia, in 1962.

Danny was inspired to take action and join the Movement. At the end of his junior year in college, in the summer of 1962, he left Chicago and headed south.

In Cairo, Illinois, he went to a church where a young black SNCC worker named John Lewis spoke. "The speech, delivered in a heavy, rural, Alabama accent, seemed to come up out of him, out of centuries of abuse, and explode with emotion," Danny remembered later. "John's speech would have converted anyone, and it converted me."

After speaking, Lewis and another Movement leader, Charles Koen, led a demonstration outside. Reporters didn't cover the demonstration. Police didn't even show up. But it was meaningful to those involved. Black and white men, women, and children marched to the town's segregated pool. They prayed together and then sang in the street. Danny watched as a blue pickup truck drove toward the protesters, forcing them to move out of the way. One brave thirteen-year-old girl refused to back down. She stayed put and let the truck knock her to the ground.

Inspired by the activists' courage, Danny went on to Atlanta, where he joined SNCC. James Forman, the organization's executive secretary, put him to work as a photographer. SNCC needed someone to take high-quality photographs to publicize the organization's activities. Danny was ready to get to work.

HISTORY IN PHOTOGRAPHS

Danny spent his summer with SNCC working to support the Civil Rights Movement in Albany, Georgia. His pictures documented what was happening in the South as well as how deeply activists felt about their mission. One photo he took at the demonstration in Cairo was used in a poster titled "Come Let Us Build a New World Together." It showed the girl who'd been knocked down by the truck praying with John Lewis and another protester.

His work was dangerous. Police commonly used violence against anyone involved in the Movement. Danny was terrified when police threw him in jail for taking pictures of the town hall. "You're shaking now, boy," a detective threatened. "You're going to be shaking a lot harder when we're done with you."

But as Danny remembers, "You wanted to be brave because other people were braver."

Danny Lyon took this photograph at the 1962 Civil Rights demonstration he attended in Cairo, Illinois. A thirteen-year-old girl who'd been knocked down during the demonstration sits and prays with other protesters, including John Lewis *(right)*.

Despite SNCC's publicity efforts, northerners didn't know much about the Civil Rights Movement yet. The media covered major events, like riots or bombings, but didn't bother with other demonstrations. "No one believed that the southern blacks . . . would rise up and fight for their rights," he said.

Danny was determined to change people's minds. Throughout his senior year at the University of Chicago, he continued traveling through the South and taking pictures that documented the Movement.

In June 1963, when Danny graduated from college, James Forman asked him to return as SNCC's official full-time staff photographer.

Danny couldn't wait to get started.

A DANGEROUS MISSION

"What do we need *him* to take our pictures for?" someone asked.

The question was rhetorical, the tone belligerent. Danny was horrified to hear it. At his first SNCC meeting as the staff photographer, he already felt out of place as a white northerner among the black members of SNCC. He knew they put their lives on the line when they demonstrated. He knew they'd been jailed over and over for their actions. And he knew what he did for the Movement—take pictures—didn't impress all of them. He was an outsider, and he wasn't taking the same risks they were.

Was he going to lose his position before he even got started?

To his relief, Danny wasn't dismissed at that first meeting. But he struggled to prove that he could make a meaningful contribution to SNCC and the Movement.

Then, in late August 1963, Forman passed along a rumor to Danny. He'd heard about a group of young girls from Americus being held prisoner at the Leesburg Stockade. Forman wanted someone to find out if the rumors were true. "Maybe you should go down there," Forman suggested to Danny. If it turned out that girls really were being held at the stockade, Forman wanted

PHOTO TECHNOLOGY IN 1963

The digital camera was invented in 1975 and wasn't commonly used until the twenty-first century. Before that, people used film cameras to take pictures. Photos taken with a film camera can't be viewed until the film inside the camera is processed, or developed. Before that, exposure to light will ruin the film.

The film is removed from the camera in total darkness in a special room called a darkroom. In the darkroom, the film is bathed and rinsed in chemicals. These chemicals change the film, so the image captured by the camera shows up. That image is called a developed negative. The negative is a reverse image of the picture that was taken.

The next step is to pass light through the negative onto photogenic paper. This creates an image on the paper that is no longer reversed. It's the picture that was taken and can finally be viewed on paper.

This photographer develops photos in a darkroom. Danny Lyon regularly used the bathroom of the Atlanta SNCC office as his darkroom.

Danny to take pictures. SNCC could share the photographic evidence with the public and with government officials, which could embarrass the local police. That might be the fastest way to get the girls released.

"For all practical purposes the girls, many as young as thirteen and all rounded up after protest marches, had been forgotten by the world, including SNCC's Atlanta office, which had its hands full," Danny later wrote. It was up to Danny to spread awareness about their situation.

He drove to the Barnum Funeral Home in Americus and learned a little more. A young black teenager knew where the stockade was located. "He says to me, 'I can take you there,'" Danny remembers. "He said, 'There's only one guard out there, an old guy named Pops. I'll keep him occupied. I'll talk to him.'"

On the spot, Danny and the teen hatched a plan.

IMMEDIATE ACTION

Danny and the teen left the funeral home and walked to the teen's car. Another African American teenager joined them. Danny climbed inside with his camera. He lay down in the well on the floor in the back and covered himself with a blanket. Off they went.

The way Danny remembers it, the ride wasn't particularly comfortable. The car jerked with every gear shift until they finally arrived at their

BREAKING STORY

News of the girls' imprisonment eventually reached a national audience when Danny's photos were published in the September 26, 1963, issue of *Jet* magazine and a 1964 issue of the *Student Voice*, SNCC's newsletter.

The *Jet* magazine article included information about other activists jailed in similar conditions. It listed the names of three SNCC workers facing the death penalty for their activism. Photos of activists who'd been beaten by police appeared in the same issue of the *Student Voice* that printed a photo of the girls at a barred window of their cell at Leesburg Stockade.

The story of what had happened to these girls did not shock the world. It was only one story among many. But gradually, all these stories added up to make Americans more aware of widespread racial injustice.

Mattie Crittenden *(left)* and Shirley Green (later Dr. Shirley Green-Reese), look at Danny through the bars of the stockade windows.

destination. The two teens got out and walked to the front of the building to distract the guard. Danny stayed in the car for a few minutes.

Was Danny scared? Not really. He was focused on his mission. "My job [was] to get something done," Danny recalls. "I [was] like a soldier."

When he guessed the coast was clear, Danny got out of the car quietly and walked up to the building. Through the window, he spotted the girls—and they saw him. He quickly explained why he was there: to take pictures of them and show the world how they were being mistreated.

A HAPPY MEETING

"What's your name?" the girls asked. "Where are you from?"

They reached through the bars to shake Danny's hand. A SNCC worker was proof the Movement hadn't forgotten them after all.

"Freedom," they said. And Danny said it too.

By then many of the girls had been at Leesburg Stockade for weeks. Lulu remembers they were simply worn out. They felt tired and wretched. When she saw Danny, she didn't know what to expect from him. She just wanted to see her parents again. She hoped his pictures could help get her out.

Danny wanted to get his work done quickly. After all, there was a guard to worry about. He didn't know if Pops had a gun.

In those first few minutes, he wasn't sure his risky mission would be a success. "I'm looking through the windows and peering into this room," Danny recalls. "The first pictures were bad."

Danny asked the girls not to crowd the window. Some of them went to the front of the room to distract the guard. The rest of the girls started re-creating how they lived, so he could capture the scenes on film. They lay on the ground to show him how they slept. They told him he should take a picture of the shower, the toilet.

"I don't think I particularly wanted to photograph a toilet with feces in it. It's not what I usually photograph," Danny says. But he knew it was important to the girls that he document what they were going through. He took the picture.

Once he was satisfied that he'd captured the girls' situation accurately, Danny wanted to get out of there. Now he *was* afraid—not for his life but for the film. He had to get his pictures safely to the outside world.

Girls posed for Danny in this photo.

The girls clustered toward the back of the cell, so there would be no reason for the guard to come up front and spot Danny outside. He went back to the car, covered himself with the blanket again, and waited for his driver to return.

"The whole thing must've taken fifteen minutes or less," Danny recalls. Then he and his teen driver left, the car lurching and bouncing on the way back to the funeral home.

Danny had to get back to the SNCC office in Atlanta. He needed to process his film.

PROOF IN PICTURES

After Danny developed his pictures, SNCC sent them to Civil Rights supporters in the North, including US senator Harrison A. Williams Jr. of New Jersey and Attorney General Robert Kennedy, President Kennedy's brother. Williams entered the pictures into the *Congressional Record*, a document that includes statements from each meeting of the House and Senate as well as other materials members may want to include. Entering the pictures didn't have legal significance and couldn't force anyone to release the girls from the Leesburg Stockade. But it did serve as proof that the federal government now knew what was happening to them.

According to many reports, when officials in Americus found out about the pictures, they acted quickly to avoid more negative publicity. By the end of August, shortly after Danny's secret photo session, Americus law enforcement finally released the girls still at the stockade. When Danny learned that the girls were free, he was thrilled. "Until that moment I don't think I had really been accepted into SNCC by some people. After all, SNCC people were activists. Most of them went to jail routinely. They *did* things. It was one of their finest qualities. All I did was make pictures," Danny wrote later. "But in Americus, my pictures had actually accomplished something. They had gotten people out of jail."

CHAPTER 7
GOING HOME

On her last day at Leesburg Stockade, Lulu Westbrook remembers being driven back to Americus in a paddy wagon. When she finally saw her mother, she hugged her and cried. In the weeks that followed, she still cried from time to time. And she liked to stay close to her mother.

Robertiena Freeman vividly remembers what happened when she and her sister Juanita finally got home after forty-five days at Leesburg Stockade.

"My mama said, 'Take your clothes off at the door.' She burned them," Robertiena recalls. "She had a hot bath and a good dinner for us."

The girls were all in rough shape, whether they'd spent weeks or days at the stockade. Emma Jean was at Leesburg Stockade for two weeks.

Billie Jo Thornton awaits her release from Leesburg Stockade.

"I was already small and had gotten skinnier. I had sores," she remembers. "[I] felt nasty. My hair was looking a mess. I was looking a mess."

Opinions varied as to what convinced officials to release various girls. Some girls from well-connected families remember their relatives putting pressure on local officials. Robertiena recalls her father working to get her and her sister out.

"I got out because my father knew the judges," Carolyn DeLoatch recalls. "He'd been before them in support of other people's children."

Lorena Barnum says her grandmother set the wheels in motion to get the girls released. "My grandmother got some judges, called the Justice Department to get us out," she says.

Most of the girls came from poor families without influential connections. Many of them credited Danny's photographic evidence with securing their freedom.

No matter when or why each girl was released, all the girls shared a sense of relief. "We got back to normal life—school, chores, playing," Lulu recalls. "Nothing had changed, but it was good to be released from prison."

THE MOVEMENT MOVES ON

The girls were finally out of jail, but their fight for freedom was far from over. Juanita still couldn't sit downstairs at the movie theater. Robertiena still had to wait for service at stores if white customers came in after her. Emma Jean couldn't get her ice cream on the white side of the Dairy Queen counter. Lorena couldn't use the dressing room at the dress shop.

Restaurants, schools, parks, and other public facilities remained segregated. Throughout the South, black Americans still struggled against oppression, racial discrimination, and violence.

By the time the girls were released, Americus was working to restore order to the city. A curfew required citizens to be home between specific hours of the night to the early morning. It was almost time for school to start again too. The city's kids were expected to get back to business as usual.

But they weren't about to give up, even after experiencing harsh consequences for their activism. Many of the girls from Leesburg Stockade kept attending mass meetings and marching in demonstrations. Many continued their activism long after the summer of 1963. The reason was simple.

"It wasn't over," Emma Jean explains. "We didn't arrive yet." Their ultimate goal, equality, was still a long way off.

BIRMINGHAM CHURCH BOMBING

Early in the school year, on September 15, 1963, a violent incident in Birmingham, Alabama, marked a turning point for the Civil Rights Movement. Members of the Ku Klux Klan bombed the 16th Street Baptist Church, a popular meeting spot for Civil Rights activists. About two hundred members were inside at the time. Four young girls—Addie Mae Collins, Carol Robertson, and Cynthia Wesley, all aged fourteen; and Denise McNair, aged eleven—were killed while waiting to attend a youth service. Fourteen others were injured.

The incident sparked riots in Birmingham and led to the deaths of more young people. Sixteen-year-old Johnny Robinson and thirteen-year-old Virgil Wade were fatally shot by police. Five hundred members of the National Guard, three hundred state troopers, five hundred police officers, and 150 sheriffs' deputies arrived to bring the city under control.

Acts of violence against black communities were nothing new. Yet the deaths of the four girls shocked and outraged the nation, bolstering support of the Civil Rights Movement.

Four KKK members were suspected of the bombing. They were not immediately charged, partly because witnesses refused to talk. Instead of going on trial, the suspects walked free for decades. Three men were eventually convicted (one in 1977, one in 2001, and one in 2002) and sentenced to life imprisonment, while the fourth suspect was never charged.

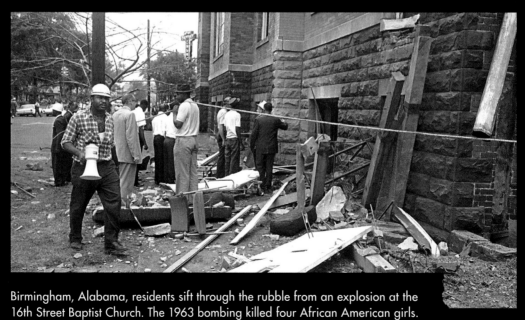

Birmingham, Alabama, residents sift through the rubble from an explosion at the 16th Street Baptist Church. The 1963 bombing killed four African American girls.

LIFE AFTER LEESBURG

Decades have passed since the girls were imprisoned at Leesburg Stockade. Their lives went in different directions after the summer of 1963. Some still live in Americus. Others moved away years ago. Some have stayed in touch, and others have drifted apart or never knew one another well. But they share the common bond of Civil Rights activists who fought for a common cause and won many victories for African Americans. Many have continued their activism.

Emma Jean Jones (Times) and Barbara Jean Daniels both remember staying with the Civil Rights Movement after getting out of Leesburg Stockade. "There were still mass meetings. It wasn't over. Something was always going on," Emma Jean says. She worried about being hit or spit on, and she knew she might be arrested again. But the possible consequences weren't enough to make her quit.

Barbara Jean felt the same way. "I continued going to meetings and marching. I didn't stop," she recalls. "I knew what I wanted. I wanted us to go to the [white] schools and have better equipment. I went for the education. I wanted better for my future. I didn't want my kid to go through what I went through."

As an adult, Barbara worked in a preschool and told her young students how important it was to get an education. "Where I came from, you got to get an education if you don't want to work for a white person," she says.

Education was a big issue for the girls who spent time at Leesburg Stockade, and although it took time, their activism did have an impact. Juanita Freeman, for example, was never allowed to attend the local white high school, Americus High, as a student. She graduated from Sumter High School, the school for black students in Americus. She went on to study at Spelman College, in Atlanta, and Georgia Southwestern State University, in Americus. But after many years as a teacher, she eventually became the principal of Americus High School in the mid-1990s. She was the first black principal there in the 115-year history of the school.

Juanita's sister, Robertiena Freeman, was one of four black students to begin integrating Americus High School in 1964. Local NAACP leaders chose her to attend. She was thrilled to have the opportunity and couldn't wait to meet her new classmates.

The experience wasn't what she'd hoped for, however. Robertiena's white classmates shoved her, spit on her, and shunned her. Her white teachers called her "the smart nigger" when she did well in class. By late fall, the other black students had returned to Sumter High School. She was the only one left at Americus High.

Robertiena stuck it out. She graduated from Americus High School in 1965 and went on to Mercer University, in Macon, Georgia.

She says she's never been invited to a high school reunion. But years after her graduation, Juanita was principal of Americus High and asked Robertiena to come for Black History Month. Robertiena agreed and had an unexpected encounter with a white former classmate. The classmate apologized personally for failing to stand up for Robertiena while they were students.

As a member of the Class of 1969, Lorena Barnum was also part of the early wave of black students who integrated Americus High School. She remembers the experience being worse than her time in Leesburg Stockade and likens it to going to war every day. But it was critical to achieving change and an important part of her activism.

"I did not give up and I did not lose my focus and I did not cave in. It was very much a defining period of my life," she says of her time in school. "It gave me the greatest confidence. If I could withstand that, I could withstand anything."

Other girls didn't attend either high school in Americus after their release from Leesburg Stockade. The family of Carolyn DeLoatch sent her to boarding school in another town. During summer breaks, she stayed involved in the

DANNY LYON

After the Civil Rights Movement, Danny continued using photography to expose difficult truths. He documented prison life in his book *Conversations with the Dead*, neighborhoods lost when the World Trade Center was built in *The Destruction of Lower Manhattan*, and Chinese industrial workers in *Deep Sea Diver*. His recent work includes the book *Burn Zone*. In 2016 his work was honored with a major retrospective exhibit, called Message to the Future, at the de Young Museum, in San Francisco, and the Whitney Museum of American Art, in New York City. He shares more about his work at https://dektol.wordpress.com.

Movement by working for the Southern Christian Leadership Conference in Atlanta. In 1968 she went to work full-time for the organization.

"I grew up in the Civil Rights Movement and became an adult and started thinking as a grown person," she says. "It changed me. It really defined my life."

Lulu Westbrook and her family moved to Rochester, New York, when she was sixteen, a few years after her arrest. Far from Americus and the southern Civil Rights Movement, she suppressed her feelings about her time in Leesburg Stockade for years. She had nightmares. She tried not to think about it. Thirty years later, she came across a book, *Memories of the Southern Civil Rights Movement*, written by Danny Lyon. She started to reflect on why she'd been involved, wrote poetry about her experiences, and began speaking publicly about her story.

PREJUDICE PERSISTS

By 1968 Civil Rights activists had won many of the rights they'd fought for. The Civil Rights Act of 1964 outlawed segregation in public places and banned employers from discriminating based on race. The Voting Rights Act of 1965 made it illegal to keep black voters from casting ballots. Restrictions such as poll taxes and literacy tests were outlawed. Black leaders were elected, even in the South.

The Civil Rights Movement of the 1960s inspired other movements that built on its legacy. In the 1960s, LGBTQ+ (lesbian, gay, bisexual, transgender, and queer/questioning) Americans began to gather support by representing themselves as a minority group that deserves equal rights. The women's rights

In the twenty-first century, activists continue to call for racial equality and justice. The grassroots group Black Lives Matter organized this 2016 demonstration in New York City. The event was officially called the Stop the Violence Rally, March, and Healing Circle.

movement also picked up ideas from the Civil Rights Movement. When women's rights leaders formed the National Organization for Women (NOW) in 1966, they followed the example of the NAACP, using similar strategies to spread their message.

Still, segregation and discrimination persist in the United States. Many who were active during the Civil Rights Movement believe it's important to recognize that equality hasn't been achieved yet. Throughout the United States, prejudice remains a reality for African Americans and for other minority groups. People face discrimination for their racial, ethnic, and religious backgrounds as well as for their gender and sexual orientation.

It is legal for private facilities to be segregated, and some communities have opened pools and clubs specifically for white people. People of color still encounter discrimination when they apply for jobs, look for housing, and try to get loans. Many schools remain only slightly integrated, and schools that have mostly students of color often have fewer resources than schools with mostly white students. Modern voting restrictions have made it harder for people of color to vote, much as literacy tests and poll taxes once did. For example, more than thirty states require voters to show photo identification at the polls. People of color are far more likely than white people to be without that type of ID.

In 2015 several prominent American politicians proposed limiting the rights of Muslims, people who practice a religion called Islam. There are approximately 1.6 billion Muslims worldwide, and many Muslims are people of color. These politicians called Muslim Americans dangerous and said their values were un-American. They stereotyped all Muslim Americans based on acts of violence committed by Muslim extremists. Some wanted to segregate Muslim immigrants from the rest of American society. Others wanted to bar Muslims from entering the country. In 2017 President Donald J. Trump began taking steps to prevent people from certain countries with large Muslim populations from entering the United States. Trump claimed this policy was not discriminatory because it was meant to keep terrorists out of the country. Thousands of Americans saw it as a Muslim ban and protested the plan.

The Trump administration also pursued policies to limit undocumented immigration from Mexico. Millions of people who had entered the United States without documentation faced arrest and deportation (removal from the country). Critics feared that strict measures against undocumented immigrants could intensify prejudice against people of color. The false idea that all Latino Americans are undocumented immigrants could lead to discrimination. For instance, law enforcement officials looking for undocumented immigrants frequently targeted Latinos and other people of color.

Prejudice persists in many forms throughout the United States. Yet the Civil Rights Movement of the 1960s offers powerful evidence that standing up against discrimination matters. The Civil Rights Movement of the 1960s won many victories, thanks to the efforts of the girls at Leesburg Stockade and thousands of others. It can continue to inspire people of all ages to work for tolerance, understanding, and equality.

I first learned about the girls who were imprisoned at Leesburg Stockade when I read an article in a 2006 issue of *Essence* magazine. I was shocked. I knew adult Civil Rights activists had been mistreated. But I didn't know much about the youngest Civil Rights activists. Their story was decades old, but it didn't feel quite like history. Most of the girls from Leesburg Stockade were still alive. I wanted to hear what they had to say about their experiences during that time. I wanted to know how these girls stood up for their rights even when they faced mistreatment and violence.

I owe a debt of gratitude to Barbara Jean Daniels, Carolyn DeLoatch, Robertiena Freeman Fletcher, Emma Pope (formerly Emma Jean Jones or Times), Lorena Barnum Sabbs, Lulu M. Westbrook Griffin, and Juanita Freeman Wilson, who were kind enough to speak with me and trust me with their stories. I am ever thankful as well to Danny Lyon, who not only took the time to talk with me but also shared his photos in this book. And a special thank-you to Sam Mahone and Teresa Mansfield, who helped put me in touch with Leesburg Stockade survivors.

Retracing history is not easy. I was not able to interview every survivor. In addition to conducting personal interviews, I used historical documents to check facts. These documents helped me discover the names of many of the girls who spent time at Leesburg Stockade and learn about the conditions there. I found information at the Americus-Sumter County Tourism Council, in Americus, Georgia, and the Albany Civil Rights Institute, in Albany, Georgia. Many of the quotes in the book were taken from affidavits housed at the Wisconsin Historical Society, in Madison, Wisconsin, which the girls gave shortly after their release. One detail of the story remains a bit mysterious. I was unable to track down paperwork about their arrests. But many of the women I spoke to said they were never officially charged with a crime.

All the women who spent time at the Leesburg Stockade deserve recognition for their courage. Their story is proof that young people can take positive action to make real and lasting change. The girls at Leesburg Stockade have earned their place in history.

1951 Sixteen-year-old Barbara Johns leads a school-wide strike to protest the unequal resources in segregated schools in Prince Edward County, Virginia.

1954 In *Brown v. Board of Education*, the US Supreme Court rules that school segregation is illegal. Southern states largely ignore this ruling.

1955 Fifteen-year-old Claudette Colvin is arrested after refusing to give up her seat to a white passenger on a segregated bus in Montgomery, Alabama.

Activist Rosa Parks refuses to give up her seat to a white rider on a Montgomery, Alabama, bus.

The black community in Montgomery begins a bus boycott to protest segregation rules on city buses.

1956 Twelve black teens integrate Clinton High School, in Clinton, Tennessee.

1957 Minnijean Brown, Elizabeth Eckford, Ernest Green, Thelma Mothershed, Melba Patillo, Gloria Ray, Terrence Roberts, Jefferson Thomas, and Carlotta Walls register as the first black students to attend Central High School, in Little Rock, Arkansas.

The Civil Rights Act of 1957 aims to stop discriminatory practices preventing black Americans from voting. The law is ignored in the South.

1960 Four black college students stage a sit-in at a "whites only" lunch counter in Greensboro, North Carolina. Similar protests follow at segregated parks, pools, theaters, libraries, and other public spaces.

Six-year-old Ruby Bridges walks through mobs of hostile white segregationists to become the first black student to attend William Frantz Elementary School, in New Orleans, Louisiana.

John F. Kennedy is elected president of the United States.

1961 CORE organizes Freedom Rides to challenge segregation practices on interstate buses. More than one thousand volunteer Freedom Riders ignore signs indicating segregated seats on buses and in waiting areas. They are confronted by violent mobs of angry white supremacists.

Martin Luther King Jr. is locked in Americus-Sumter County jail, along with Ralph D. Abernathy, a cofounder of the Southern Christian Leadership Committee, and Dr. William G. Anderson, an Americus native and the president of the Albany Movement.

1962 James Meredith enrolls at the University of Mississippi as the first black student. Federal troops escort him in to protect him from a white mob.

Malcolm X becomes the national spokesperson of the Nation of Islam, an African American religious movement. His philosophy runs counter to the Movement's. He urges African Americans to fight for equality "by any means necessary," including violence.

1963 Martin Luther King Jr. is arrested in Birmingham for demonstrating without a city permit. He writes "Letter from a Birmingham Jail" to explain his actions to those who question his methods and the importance of the Movement.

President John F. Kennedy delivers a speech to the nation in support of Civil Rights.

Medgar Evers, Mississippi's high-profile NAACP field secretary, is shot and killed by a white separatist.

President Kennedy is assassinated.

1964 Malcom X leaves the Nation of Islam.

President Lyndon Johnson signs the Civil Rights Act of 1964, which outlaws segregation.

1965 Johnson speaks publicly against the Ku Klux Klan, calling them terrorists.

Malcolm X is assassinated.

A peaceful march for voting rights from Selma to Montgomery, Alabama, is met with violence from police.

Congress passes the Voting Rights Act of 1965, which bans discriminatory practices that prevent black people from voting.

1968 Martin Luther King is assassinated.

Johnson signs the Civil Rights Act of 1968, which outlaws discrimination in the sale, rental, and financing of housing.

SOURCE NOTES

Unless otherwise noted here, quotes used in this book are taken from personal interviews with the author.

5 Freedom Summer Collection, Wisconsin Historical Society, Madison, Wisconsin, King—SNCC Position Papers & Reports, 1963–1965 (Mary E. King papers, 1962–1999; Z: Accessions, M82-445, Box 1, Folder 20).

14 "Examples of Jim Crow Laws," *The Jackson Sun*, http://www.ferris.edu /jimcrow/links/misclink/examples /homepage.htm.

20 "The Limits of Nonviolence," *Eyes on the Prize, American Experience, PBS*, August 23, 2006, http://www.pbs.org /wgbh/amex/eyesontheprize/story /06_albany.html.

21 Joe Holley, "Civil Rights Leader James Forman Dies," *Washington Post*, January 11, 2005, http://www .washingtonpost.com/wp-dyn/articles /A1621-2005Jan11.html.

25 Glenn M. Robins, "Americus Movement," New Georgia Encyclopedia, last modified by NGE staff, December 3, 2013, http://www .georgiaencyclopedia.org/articles /history-archaeology/americus -movement.

28 Freedom Summer Collection, Wisconsin Historical Society.

29 Ibid.

30 "The Civil Rights History Project: Survey of Collections and Repositories," American Folklife Center, Library of Congress, accessed October 13, 2016, http://www.loc.gov /folklife/civilrights/survey/view_ collection.php?coll_id=2653.

30 "An Appeal to All Citizens of Americus and Sumter County, Deposition; Henrietta Fuller; Deposition; Eliza Thomas; Deposition; Lorine Sanders; Deposition; Robertiena Freeman; Deposition; Lorena Barnum; Deposition; Emma Jean Times," King—SNCC Position Papers & Reports, 1963–1965 (except Waveland, Mississippi, November 1964) (Mary E. King papers, 1962–1999; Z: Accessions, M82-445, Box 1, Folder 20), Wisconsin Historical Society, Freedom Summer Collection, http://content.wisconsinhistory.org/cdm /ref/collection/p15932coll2/id/24757.

31 Freedom Summer Collection, Wisconsin Historical Society.

31 Ibid.

35 "An Appeal to All Citizens," King— SNCC Position Papers.

35 Ibid.

35–36 Ibid.

36 Ibid.

37 Ibid.

38 "Message from James Farmer about March on Washington for Jobs and Freedom," August 28, 1963, available online at King Center, http://www .thekingcenter.org/archive/document /message-james-farmer-about-march -washington-jobs-and-freedom.

39 "An Appeal to All Citizens," King— SNCC Position Papers.

39 Ibid.

41 Danny Lyon, *Memories of the Southern Civil Rights Movement* (Santa Fe, NM: Twin Palms, 2010), 24.

41 Ibid.

42 Ibid., 42.

44 Ibid., 80.

45 Ibid.

45 Ibid.

47 Ibid.

GLOSSARY

affidavit: an official statement

"colored": a term for black people, adopted in the nineteenth century; considered offensive in the twenty-first century

Confederate: someone who supported the southern states that attempted to leave the United States, sparking the Civil War (1861–1865)

discrimination: unfair treatment based on race

inequality: difference in the amount or type of something; a situation in which some people have advantages that others do not

integration: mixing people of different races

lynch: to murder, usually by hanging, often with a large group of supporters present

minority: a group that is not as large or powerful in a society as another group

Negro: a term for black people that became standard in the early twentieth century and became less common in the late twentieth century; in the twenty-first century, considered offensive by some

"nigger": a slur for black people, used to express contempt and hate; considered offensive since the nineteenth century

people of color: people who do not identify as white, such as people of African American, Latin American, American Indian, or Asian descent

race: a group of people who share distinctive physical traits, such as skin color

segregation: the practice of separating people of different races

shotgun shack: a small house in which the rooms are organized one behind another in a line

Southern Christian Leadership Conference (SCLC): an African American Civil Rights organization founded in 1957 by activists including Martin Luther King Jr. and Ella Baker

stockade: an enclosure, often used to confine animals or people

Student Nonviolent Coordinating Committee (SNCC): an African American Civil Rights organization founded in 1957 by Ella Baker

SELECTED BIBLIOGRAPHY

"Americus," Freedom on Film: Civil Rights in Georgia, University of Georgia. Accessed October 2, 2016. http://www.civilrights.uga.edu/bibliographies/americus.

"An Appeal to All Citizens of Americus and Sumter County, Deposition; Henrietta Fuller; Deposition; Eliza Thomas; Deposition; Lorine Sanders; Deposition; Robertiena Freeman; Deposition; Lorena Barnum; Deposition; Emma Jean Times." King—SNCC Position Papers & Reports, 1963–1965 (except Waveland, Mississippi, November 1964) (Mary E. King papers, 1962–1999; Z: Accessions, M82-445, Box 1, Folder 20), Wisconsin Historical Society, Freedom Summer Collection. http://content.wisconsinhistory.org/cdm/ref /collection/p15932coll2/id/24757.

"The Civil Rights History Project: Survey of Collections and Repositories." American Folklife Center, Library of Congress. Accessed October 3, 2016. http://www.loc.gov/folklife /civilrights/survey/view_collection.php?coll_id=2653.

Collins, Genie. "Recalling the Civil Rights Movement of 1963 in Americus." *Americus Times-Recorder,* February 26, 2007. http://www.americustimesrecorder.com/news/local_news /recalling-the-civil-rights-movement-of-in-americus/article_0daf1fa3-acaa-5185-8dd1 -c51f1e6e3acf.html.

"Ga. Marchers Kept in Filthy, Stench-Filled Jail." *Jet,* September 26, 1963, 23–25.

Green-Reese, Shirley. "Untold Story: Justice Denied, the 1963 Americus-Sumter Civil Rights Movement Americus, Georgia." Accessed October 3, 2016. http://www.crmvet.org/info /leesburg.htm.

Jim Crow Museum of Racist Memorabilia, Ferris State University, Big Rapids, Michigan. Accessed October 3, 2016. http://www.ferris.edu/HTMLS/news/jimcrow/location.htm.

Kohut, Andrew. "JFK's America." Pew Research Center, November 20, 2013. http://www .pewresearch.org/fact-tank/2013/11/20/jfks-america.

"The Limits of Nonviolence." *Eyes on the Prize, American Experience, PBS,* August 23, 2006. http://www.pbs.org/wgbh/amex/eyesontheprize/story/06_albany.html.

"Local Black History Chronology." Compiled by Alan Anderson. *Americus Times-Recorder,* February 7, 2008. http://www.americustimesrecorder.com/i-local-black-history -chronology-i/article_9a41ffc7-a3ae-5a52-8956-75eb1edc5f37.html.

Lyon, Danny. *Memories of the Southern Civil Rights Movement.* Santa Fe, NM: Twin Palms, 2010.

"Message from James Farmer about March on Washington for Jobs and Freedom," August 28, 1963. Available online at the King Center. http://www.thekingcenter.org/archive /document/message-james-farmer-about-march-washington-jobs-and-freedom.

"Notes on the Civil Rights Protest Era in Americus, Ga." Compiled by Alan Anderson. *Americus Times-Recorder.* Accessed October 3, 2016. http://www.sumtercountyhistory .com/history/CIVILRTS.htm.

Owens, Donna. "Stolen Girls." *Essence*, June 2006. http://www.essence.com/2008/09/09 /stolen-girls.

Shaffer, Graham P. "Student Works, the Leesburg Stockade Girls: Why Modern Legislatures Should Extend the Statue of Limitations for Specific Jim-Crow-Era Reparations Lawsuits in the Wake of Alexander v. Oklahoma." *Stetson Law Review*, Spring 2008. https:// litigation-essentials.lexisnexis.com/webcd/app?action=DocumentDisplay&crawlid =1&doctype=cite&docid=37+Stetson+L.+Rev.+941&srctype=smi&srcid=3B15&key =388ed10f208903cba8f2b73b28b23e27.

"Stolen Girls Remember 1963 in Leesburg." *WALB News*, July 24, 2006. http://www.walb .com/story/5190050/stolen-girls-remember-1963-in-leesburg.

Student Nonviolent Coordinating Committee. *Student Voice*, 1960–1965. Compiled by the staff of the Martin Luther King, Jr., Papers Project, Clayborne Carson, senior editor and director.

FURTHER INFORMATION

Hoose, Phillip. *Claudette Colvin: Twice toward Justice*. New York: Melanie Kroupa Books, 2009. Read about a teenage Civil Rights activist whose bravery on an Alabama bus was forgotten for decades.

Huey, Lois Miner. *Forgotten Bones*. Minneapolis: Millbrook Press, 2015. Learn the secrets of a recently discovered slave cemetery in upstate New York and find out more about slavery's legacy.

Levinson, Cynthia. *We've Got a Job: The 1963 Birmingham Children's March*. Atlanta: Peachtree, 2012. Learn how children and teens filled the streets and the jails of Birmingham, Alabama, in the name of Civil Rights.

Lewis, John, Andrew Aydin, and Nate Powell. *March: Book One*. Marietta, GA: Top Shelf, 2013.

———. *March: Book Two*. Marietta, GA: Top Shelf, 2015.

———. *March: Book Three*. Marietta, GA: Top Shelf, 2016. In this graphic nonfiction trilogy, Congressman John Lewis shares how he went from poor sharecropper to Civil Rights leader.

Lowery, Lynda Blackmon. *Turning 15 on the Road to Freedom*. New York: Dial, 2015. Lynda Blackmon Lowery, the youngest voting rights marcher at Selma in 1965, tells her story of fighting for equality and justice as a teenager.

Rubin, Susan Goldman. *Freedom Summer: The 1964 Struggle for Civil Rights in Mississippi*. New York: Holiday House, 2014. Hear how Civil Rights activists struggled for their cause despite threats, violence, and even murder.

INDEX

PHOTO ACKNOWLEDGMENTS

The images in this book are used with the permission of: Design: © iStockphoto.com/
Ladida (grunge border); © iStockphoto.com/CristianIoan (brick design); Backgrounds:
© iStockphoto.com/Vladimirovic (gray wall); Everett Collection/Newscom, p. 4; © Danny
Lyon/Magnum Photos, Courtesy Gavin Brown Enterprises, pp. 6, 28, 31, 32, 34, 36, 40,
42, 45, 46, 48; © Laura Westlund/Independent Picture Service, p. 7; © Paul Schutzer/
Getty Images, p. 8; IanDagnall Computing/Alamy Stock Photo, p. 10; © Buyenlarge/
Archive Photos/Getty Images, p. 12; Everett Collection Historica/Alamy Stock Photo, p. 3;
© Robert W. Kelley/Time Life Pictures/Getty Images, p. 15; © H. Armstrong Roberts/
Retrofile/Getty Images, p. 16; The Granger Collection, New York, pp. 19, 21 (bottom), 25;
© Afro American Newspapers/Gado/Getty Images, p. 21 (top); © Bettmann Archive/Getty
Images, p. 23; AP Photo/Bill Hudson, p. 24; © Bettmann Archive/Getty Images, p. 27;
Library of Congress (LC-DIG-ppmsca-03128), p. 37; © Bettmann Archive/Getty Images,
p. 38; Arthur Tanner/Fox Photos/Getty Images, p. 43; AP Photo, p. 50; © Erik McGregor/
Pacific Press/LightRocket/Getty Images, p. 54.

Front cover: © Danny Lyon/Magnum Photos, Courtesy Gavin Brown Enterprises;
© iStockphoto.com/Ladida (grunge border); © iStockphoto.com/Vladimirovic (gray wall).

Back cover: © iStockphoto.com/CristianIoan (brick design); © iStockphoto.com/Ladida
(grunge border).